Your Healthy Cell

Optimizing Health,
Brain Cells to Stem Cells

To Beverly,
Here's to a healthier
future!

Best,
Reg[?] [signature]

Your Healthy Self

Optimizing Health,
Brain Cells to Stem Cells

Regan Archibald, Lac, CSSAc, FMP

YouSpeakIt
PUBLISHING
The Easy Way
to Get Your Book
Done Right™

I dedicate this book to all of you amazing people on the planet who are creating a bigger future for yourselves and for the generations to come. This is for those who are pushing the limits in life and love, and to those who leave the earth a little bit better than the way that they found it.

Your Healthy Self is a book dedicated to help you love the way you feel about your health. *Your healthy self* can simply be broken down into *heal thy self*. Loving the way you feel about your health gives you confidence in your future and allows you to invest more fully in your career, your relationships, and your family. That means you have pain-free living, a rejuvenated brain, habits to cultivate 120-year-old healthy life, and constant stem cell replenishment. Living with pain and chronic disease is not loving the way you feel about your health.

When you become aware of how to best care for yourself, you start to love the way you feel about your health and about your life. Most of us have no idea how to take care of ourselves, and we have struggled with fatigue, emotional stress, hormonal dysregulation, digestive issues, and brain fog and have no clue how to get out of pain to get our bodies moving again.

My hope is this book will give you some of the answers you seek on your path to becoming a healthier version of yourself.

Contents

Acknowledgments

I would like to acknowledge first and foremost my wife, Jessica. She is an endless source of inspiration, encouragement, and love for me. I cannot believe how lucky I am to have such a phenomenal woman in my life. Not only does she pick me up when I am stuck, but she also provides incredible insights for understanding my own capabilities and talents so that I can show up as the best version of myself and serve in more meaningful ways.

I want to thank my two boys, Jonah and Dominic, for challenging me to get super fit before I turned forty. It has been a nice journey to decrease my body fat low enough to have my abdominal muscles stick out again. I want to thank them for their creativity and for keeping me young and wanting to stay healthy so that I can enjoy their entire lives. I also want to thank my daughter, Zoe, whose personality and sense of humor keeps me laughing and for our deep connection and love.

I want to thank all the members of the Go Wellness family who constantly push me to think outside of the box and for the inspiration and zest for life that they bring. I could not ask for a better group of healthcare transformers. I love the fun and energy that we create together.

I thank all the individuals at East West Health who have created an incredible practice model that is setting the trends for the future of medicine and setting the bar high in how healthcare can be delivered and how to improve the experience of our patients. I appreciate every single one of the members of my team who have helped facilitate the ushering in of a new medical model.

I wish to acknowledge and show appreciation for the stem cell researchers that have gone before me such as Arnold Caplan, PhD, Neil Roidan, PhD, Robert Hariri, MD, and Eliott Spencer, PhD. I also acknowledge all the scientists and researchers who are bringing this incredible medicine into the clinics. We now have a ground-breaking opportunity in healthcare, and I appreciate all the work that has been done.

And lastly, I appreciate the source of life, creativity, and wisdom. I am deeply grateful that I have an opportunity to be connected to that source whenever I call on it.

Introduction

With a simple shift in spacing, *Healthy Self* becomes *Heal Thy Self*. My mission is to end pain and chronic disease for one million people by 2025. The only way I can pull this off is by motivating the amazing people I work with to take their health to the next level and *heal themselves* daily.

Your Healthy Self is about expanding the way that you look at your health and your life. It is about challenging your way of thinking about your health. This book will take you on a journey where you will be able to see that *health and healing is a transformative process that can be multiplied every single day.*

Imagine if you could improve your health just 1 percent per day for 100 days.

You would achieve a 100 percent health improvement, right?

Amazing to think about. This is the process that we have coached thousands of people just like you with remarkable results. Do not think big, think small when it comes to removing obstacles that are getting in the way of your health.

This book will explore the number one cause of death—*aging*. It will explain the truth that aging is a disease, regardless of what the FDA, the AMA, or the CDC say about it. Aging is the cause of death for over 100,000 people daily worldwide. I hope you will experience exponential growth in your health so that you can live a long, healthy, and abundant life. I hope you live not only a life that serves you and gives you the meaning and depth that you come to know and love, but also a life that allows you to serve deeper and connect with others in more meaningful ways.

This book will help you understand ways of reversing the degenerative and destructive processes of aging—specifically, biological aging. I cannot do anything to stop the sun or the earth's orbit for your chronological age, but I am going to give you some great tips for changing your biological age in this book. The other thing that I am going to explore with you is how to turn on your brain in new ways regardless of any damage that you feel you have been subjected to. Patients of ours who have explored a healing journey with stem cell therapy for their brain have been able to move again, have conversations again, and their brains have turned on like they've never experienced before.

I will also share stories with you to help motivate and inspire you to make some radical changes in the way you start your day—to create greater levels of health. These changes can be as simple as taking a few deep breaths or writing down what you are grateful for. If you can create one great day in your life, then you can create an amazing life.

I will share with you the traps we fall into when we feel like there is a scarcity of health and no opportunities beyond the drugs or surgical options that many of you have been given. I want to shine light on a new path and the future of medicine that has arrived. Good news, the future is here.

I hope this book becomes a long-term source of inspiration for you, and please know that this book can be read in whatever way you like. Start at the end or start at the new research, I have found that my own life has transformed to the place where I feel stronger, healthier, and happier than ever before. This knowledge has been a true gift to me, and I believe that any time that life gives you a gift, your responsibility is to give that gift to others.

I wrote this book to empower people with *real health solutions* no matter what diagnosis they've been given. Your healthier future is here, and I feel like I did not have a choice but to send this message out. This book is my gift to you! I wrote it to shine a light on a path for your life, and maybe you can find some inspiration to take your life and health to the next level.

Once you have health independence, everything else comes to life. This is the place where you can be more creative and learn how to have financial independence, great relationships, and an abundance of purpose. It is also a place where you find which ways you can serve deeper and develop better new talents.

If you can create a little bigger and slightly better future for yourself and those around you, then I've succeeded. I also wrote this book because I believe that right now humanity needs direction. We need more leaders who stand up and point to a direction that leads to health independence.

This book took a lot of courage to release to you. Some of the data in here will be somewhat controversial. I hope that you will do your due diligence and, if there are things that do not necessarily apply to you or do not resonate with you, then shelf them for now. But, come back and look at it later. There may be another point in your life when you will be ready to embrace the new breakthroughs that I will be sharing in this book.

One thing that I would recommend is to have a pen ready. Mark up your book. I have done this with the books that have contributed the most for me in my life. The best way that I have found to get the most out of books is to take lots of notes within the book's pages, and then apply these as quickly as I possibly can.

Creating a journal or an action plan is another great way that you can experiment and find out if the information in this book is helpful for you. At the very least, I hope you enjoy it. I hope you can sit down with a nice warm cup of coffee or tea with this book, and it creates some excitement in your life. Thank you for reading it. The final thing that I would recommend is to also read my first book *Your Health Transformation*. This book provides many details on detoxification and gut health. It will give you some practical solutions behind the concepts contained in this book.

Many of you have heard me talk or make presentations on health, have been to my webinars, or listened to my podcasts. And, many of you have read other books that I have written, but this book is based on some the newest research that I have uncovered, some of which is contrary to things I have learned in the past.

Start in the beginning, the middle, or read wherever you like. That is how I read books, so this is not meant to be a chapter by chapter book. Read this book in the manner that you find works best for your brain.

Your brain loves novelty and challenge. This book will show you ways that you can improve your brain and create some excitement for a bigger future. The biggest thing that I hope you will gain from this book is what we call *exponential health*. This is where you are multiplying your health every day by all the small things you do. Exponential health comes when you make the simple shift of a 1 percent improvement in your health every day.

The small things that multiply health can be as simple as:

- Smiling more often
- Taking six deep breaths to change your mindset
- Moving your body more and exercising
- Finding people to connect with on a deeper level
- Cultivating the relationships that mean the most to you
- Taking on bigger challenges

I believe this book will serve as a foundation to build your future on. I want to help you live to be 250 and beyond with the incredible breakthroughs in medicine that are becoming available. In the Next Steps section at the end of the book, you will find my website where you can jump into my 5-day or 100-day challenge.

I appreciate you joining me on this journey and allowing me to express my deeper meaning and purpose in life, which is to end pain and chronic disease for as many people as I possibly can in my lifetime. I hope that you will gain deeper appreciation for the beautiful physical body that you have, and the incredible enlightened brain that is between your ears, and your big wide-open heart that can hug the entire planet.

> *From the moment I stepped through the door at East West Health, I was met with genuine, professional, knowledgeable, and concerned people. Every aspect of the process was explained and performed perfectly. In short, I could not be happier with my decision, and I am confident that because of their work my life has dramatically been changed for the better!*
>
> ~ Chris L

CHAPTER ONE

Game Plan to Extend Life and Health

CHOOSING WHEN YOU DIE

How Long Do You Want to Live?

I imagine that if you and I were sitting down together and sharing stories about our lives, we'd have a lot in common. You and I would probably agree that life gives us exactly what we need to grow. However, no matter how we look at it, we still get caught off guard and resist the process.

Maybe you've received a diagnosis of a chronic disease or had some debilitating pain show up from an old injury you now must deal with. Maybe you discovered that you are, in fact, older than you thought as you are renewing your driver's license. In your mind, you tell yourself: *You can't win 'em all.*

What makes your life unique?

The frustration you feel turns to despair, and you forget just how amazing you are. The reality is that you have an incredible gift to offer the world. The people in your life now and in the future benefit more than you could ever imagine by you being you. Whatever struggles you are going through now are the material you need to become a newer, upgraded, healthier you.

We resist this reality—okay, I resist this reality all the time. Remember, no matter where we are in life, we need challenges to grow. It's all part of living. The toughest trees are the ones that survive in the harshest conditions. Some of the most expressive trees that I've seen in my life are on the windswept ridges of Kohala on the Big Island of Hawaii. These trees are twisted, misshapen, and have a serious lean to them because of their environment, but they are absolutely gorgeous—just like you. My favorite people in the world are like these trees. It's the struggles that make us unique and make us who we are.

Keep in mind that we've done a great job creating convenience in our lives so that we can avoid any opposition. Even simple recommendations I make—like taking a cold shower every morning for better adrenal health—are met with wide-eyed panic. It's only two minutes of discomfort that can lead to hours of increased energy, but because it's not easy, we won't do it.

Why is this?

At our core, we want comfort and certainty, but if you are in the process of extending your life and waking up to your healthiest self, you will want to embrace all the challenges that come your way. You crave certainty in your environment, your work, and especially in your health, but forget that there's little growth in certainty. It's the small doses of uncertainty that expand your life and your health. This uncertainty is as energizing as it is daunting, but without it, life would be pretty dull.

Why would we want to live another day if we had all the answers?

I am so grateful that I have one of my grandmothers still alive. Her name is Verla Archibald, and she's one of the most incredible women you could ever meet. Even in her eighties, she can still outwork most of us who are half her age. Her secret might be the Idaho farm that she has pride in, her multiple woodworking projects, or her deeper connection to her family and relationships. Maybe it's all that. She's a leader to all of us, and I hope she lives many more decades. Every day, Grandma Verla gets up and completes her work for the day without complaints or expectations that someone will do it for her. She lives for the day at hand and prepares for a long future.

The saying: *Live every day as if it's your last* is great advice, but *Live as if you will live forever* is equally as compelling.

I've noticed that the people in my life who live each day to the fullest have the mindset that life is fun and worth living. Too many people limit their lives; they see others around them dying at the age of seventy-five or eighty and shrug it off. Perhaps you have you gone to your doctor and she's told you: *It's because of your age.*

What if you started looking at aging as a process that could be reversed?

What if you could get *younger* as you aged?

From what I've seen, there are many cases of people living well beyond the normal defined lifespan, and this book will explore some ways that you can do the same.

The questions you need to answer are:

- How long do you want to live?

- Would you live to be 120 if you could?

- What are the greatest ways that you could cultivate a bigger, healthier, and better future for yourself and the ones you love?

Make Every Year Better

The Pew Research Center asked Americans whether they would use technologies that could allow them to live 120 years or beyond. The results were 56 percent said: *No, they wouldn't.* Many of these people aren't opposed to using medications or life support, which are also technologies, but they wouldn't use cellular medicine or computerized assistance.

One of my greatest mentors in life is Dan Sullivan. He is the founder of Strategic Coach. One of the things that I found the most intriguing about him is his goal to live to the year 2100, or the age of 156. He was born May 19, 1944 and simply wants to live through an entire, uninterrupted century. Dan Sullivan has been on my podcast, Go Wellness Radio, and has inspired many of my patients and thousands of his clients to think differently about their age.

The way that Dan Sullivan thinks about the future is that every year will continually get better. He believes that if you have freedom of time, freedom of purpose, freedom of relationships, and freedom of money, then there is no reason to die at the typical eighty-year-old mark. His current process is based on twenty-five-year increments where he considers the future and creates a strategy to make every year better. I see Dan every three months in Toronto, and each time I see him, he looks more energetic, more fit, and more ambitious than the time before. He has the mindset along with a solid plan to reach his aging goal.

Winning the Aging Game

Aging is a disease. It is the number one cause of death on the planet and kills over 100,000 people every single day. Worldwide, 52,000 people die of natural causes, but 100,000 deaths occur every day from aging—making it the leading cause of death, ahead of heart disease, cancer, and obesity. Understanding that every disease process has an aging process, or degeneration of healthy function in our bodies, is what can liberate your ability to live a long life.

When you start looking at aging as a disease process then you can discover the underlying causes and address them. When you can discover *why* your body ages, then you can create a strategy around *what* to do about it. And, if you don't know what to do, keep reading.

Aging is finally getting some much-needed perspective by the World Health Organization (WHO). The WHO defines healthy aging as, "the process of developing and maintaining the functional ability that enables wellbeing in older age." Functional ability is about having the capabilities that enable all people to be and do what they have reason to value.

This includes a person's ability to:

- Meet basic needs
- Learn, grow, and choose
- Have mobility
- Build and maintain relationships
- Contribute to society

Winning the game of aging is all about finding the gaps in your health, mindset, and emotions and then bridging the gaps with new habits and behaviors. Once you've implemented those habits and lifestyle changes, the momentum will allow you to create your new future. Momentum is the building block for future health and reversal of aging.

The biggest thing you must watch out for is being hit by a car or by the tail of a whale, like one of my patients did. I was shocked when Janet was wheeled into my office full of bruises from her accident. While she was snorkeling near Dominica, the tail of a whale struck her. She was with her husband, daughter, and son-in-law. The tail of a forty-three-foot mother whale just brushed Janet and nearly killed her. She has always been focused on promoting her own health and longevity, and this accident nearly killed her. But fortunately, she recovered.

Janet came into the clinic multiple times over the course of the next few months, and we nursed her back to health. But, those accidents are what can take us out sooner than we would like. So, mitigating risk is another piece of winning the game on aging.

Incredible Asset to Humankind

I attended my wife's great-grandmother's one-hundredth birthday party. To see somebody like Grandma Wilson, who has the wit, charm, and intelligence of most people half her age, is inspiring. She is someone who grew up without electricity. She grew up without vehicles—just a horse and buggy. She has not traveled much throughout her life, but she has seen dramatic changes in the landscape of the world.

I asked Grandma Wilson what the most impactful technology or change that she's seen throughout her life was. She said that the internet is the biggest thing that is a mystery to her in how it connects so many people around the world. The other thing that is important to realize is that Grandma Wilson not only has inspired her entire posterity, she has created many meaningful relationships. She has people she's connected with, and people who rely on her.

No matter what age you are, you are a huge asset to humankind because of the relationships you have created. Not only are you inspiring other people and helping humanity when you keep yourself healthy, but you are also out there doing good and moving things forward because you provide a context of the past. You hold a window for all of us to look through and experience the way life was in the past, so we can create more meaning and understanding about how to create a better future.

I witness life becoming more and more exciting. The future appears more and more impressive.

WHY DO WE AGE?

I think understanding why we age gives us an opportunity to confront the biggest obstacles that stand in our way, such as inflammation, lifestyle choices, and lack of connection with other people. Understanding the physiological process of aging is one of the key ingredients that allows you to create habits and choices so that you are not a victim of this thing we call aging.

In the fifteen years that I've been practicing, one of the most disturbing trends that I've noticed is the amount of people who are stuck between life and death. So much so, that we now have a term for this called *premature mortality*, and the ramifications are sobering. I do not want this to happen to you.

Premature mortality is like walking around with a skeleton mask on. You cast the image of death, but from what we can see, you are living based on the fact that you are moving, breathing, talking, and relating. According to the Organisation for Economic Cooperation and Development, premature mortality is "measured in terms of potential years of life lost (PYLL) before the age of seventy years." Heart attacks, cancer, diabetes, and brain injuries are now more common than ever and have left many people dead amongst the living. Last year the Lancet reported that 95 percent of people worldwide have at least one chronic disease. What's worse is the treatments for chronic disease are still drugs and surgery.

Think about your health and your life—how are you doing?

Are you falling victim to premature mortality and chronic disease, or will you fight back and bypass the statistics?

If its not you, then I bet that there's someone in your life who is struggling. They might be your neighbor, family member, co-worker, or that one friend you just ran into at the gym or store.

Aging is the final function of cellular death. When our cells die off without replacement, this is called *senescence*. Once the lineage of cell is gone, aging and disease set in. The more cellular lineages die, the older we become. Many of you have cartilage that is gone in your knees or hips. Once the cartilage cells are gone, you end up with aging and disease in that joint because the cartilage cells aren't going to regrow on their own. This is senescence. It's degeneration and can happen anywhere in your body.

So, how can we regenerate cells that are deteriorated?

Cells can regenerate through tissue allographs or *stem cell therapy*. Stem cells are the master cells in our body that are there to repair damage from aging. And, if we can use stem cell therapy to replace these damaged or aged cells in your joints, then we have possibly cornered aging because we can also use the same therapy for your heart, lungs, or even brain.

With regenerative medicine breakthroughs, we've got a leg up on aging. This is one of the miracle breakthroughs that will soon allow us all to thrive regardless of our chronological age.

Reversing Cellular Death

Every minute you lose 300 million cells—yes, 300 million. The amount of cellular death that occurs in your body stands in the way of living a long, healthy life. If your cells keep dying, then what eventually happens to you? You die. Otherwise, no big deal, right?

One of the key components to stopping this aging process is making sure that we have enough cells to repopulate the cells that are dying every second, every minute, every hour of every day. The best way for our bodies to maintain cellular health is by having the right nutrition, hormones, and digestive health. Health in each of these systems will allow us to have healthy stem cells to repopulate the cells that are dying off. Having the proper proliferation and regeneration of stem cells in our bodies is what researchers are finding will reverse cellular death.

What is aging, anyway?

What is disease?

The definition of aging is poor regeneration or degeneration of organs and tissues. Disease is a departure from the functional aspects of the organs in your body. So, if you consider these two definitions of aging and disease, they are synonymous. If you stop disease in your body, you stop aging.

Function is the ability to perform an action. Your body will be 100 percent healthy if you have 100 percent function and proper cellular turnover and health. Symptoms are simply the manifestation of mal-functions that have led to disease and aging. Symptoms are what you experience every day with pain, stomachaches, or poor sleep. These things aren't the cause; they are the check engine light, telling you something is wrong.

Rituals to Hang Your *Aging* Hat On

In life, you are making choices to move away from pain or towards pleasure. Like it or not, you create both happiness and misery in your life. If you can decide to be happy every day, then you will live a life without feeling old. Happiness allows you to see in your mind's eye a future that can always be expanded. When you are creating a continual process of visualizing, experiencing, and enjoying a bigger future you are adding to the health in your body. It changes your vibration and improves your momentum away from aging.

I like to start every morning doing Qi Gong and vigorous breathing. Wim Hoff, the *Iceman*, teaches a powerful breathing technique of inhaling deeply and exhaling completely thirty times, and then holding your breath for one to two minutes, or as long as you can. (wimhofmethod. com) Feel free to try it. I will wait for you.

Did you notice how your hands felt tingly?

Did you feel a bit light-headed?

These sensations are from completely oxygenating your body. Research shows that this will make your blood more alkaline. If you do this several times per day, you will have a much easier time staying happy, healthy, and motivated. If you want to step it up a notch, do this breathing technique at the end of your shower, but turn the water to cold. Yes, cold!

Simply breathe through the resistance of the cold water, and you will feel a rush of epinephrine that will give you enormous energy throughout your day. It's also a great coffee substitute. Too many people are addicted to the morning coffee ritual, and if you can push your coffee consumption to later in the day, you will have better energy, feel more grounded, and protect your adrenal glands. Just don't forget to add some fats like medium-chain triglyceride (MCT) oil, ghee, or grass-fed butter into your coffee so that the caffeine is released in a sustainable way.

Daily meditation, visualization, and affirmations keep me focused on the positives in my life and enhance the vibrations and energy in my body. One of my dear patients is phenomenal at entering this deep meditative state. When I talk to her, I notice she is far more present than other people

I speak to. She has a greater capacity for making a connection with those around her. She makes meditation a daily part of her life. This is one of the keys to being healthy—staying connected and experiencing the pleasure that comes from your life.

It's easy to live a life full of distractions. Unfortunately, the distractions create more stress in our brains, our amygdala expands, and we go into a *fight-or-flight* mode. When the amygdala grows, we get stuck in this negative repetitious cycle where we cannot transition and transform out of the disease process. This is where unnecessary aging comes from. And, the lack of the moving in the right direction is one of the reasons we have cellular death.

Once more, cold showers are your portal to becoming more alert, having better blood circulation, and healthier adrenal glands. If you can get in the habit of spending the final two minutes of your showers on cold, you will experience healthier skin, and an increase of dopamine throughout your day. Enjoy!

Action Plan:

- Thirty full inhalations and exhalations while taking a cold bath or shower

- Save your coffee until 11 a.m. or noon

- Practice moving your body with Qi Gong or Yoga upon waking

- Use meditation and visualization

- Choose to be happy every day

Brain Makeover With Cellular Medicine

A research article published in the journal, *Nature,* showed that hypothalamic stem cells influence aging. Researchers discovered that when mice started to show signs of aging their neural (brain) hypothalamic stem cells started to diminish in numbers. They found they could predict the aging of mice based on these neural stem cells. When they were depleted, the mice aging process would accelerate.

To test their hypothesis, researchers created a virus to target and destroy the neural stem cells in the hypothalamus of the brains of the mice. When the virus was introduced into the eight- to ten-months-old mice, they became *old* mice that took on characteristics of twenty to twenty-four-month-old mice—most mice live to be around twenty-four months.

The researchers then hypothesized: if they could reverse aging by introducing stem cells into the mice, would the mice regain their youthfulness and vitality? And, sure enough, the mice that received stem cells back into their hypothalamus, reduced their signs of aging. This was true not only in the younger mice that had the viral implant, but also in the older mice. The mice became young again just by introducing stem cells.

This begs the question for you and me that if we can introduce young, healthy stem cells from perinatal tissue into our brains, will it reverse aging?

Of course, we can never just look at one piece of research and conclude that we've got it all figured out, but I think this research gives us a great place to start. So, let's look at how can we safely and effectively enhance the aging function in our brain. One of the primary ways that we have safely treated the brain is with an intranasal SphenoCath applicator. Sounds odd, and yes, it feels odd, but after receiving this procedure, I am sleeping better, my hearing and sight have improved, and my sense of smell has been enhanced as has taste. My brain has felt much more organized, and I also have noticed better overall strength and cardiovascular health.

I grew up having experienced several concussions in sports and on motorcycles. The intranasal procedure seems to have reorganized my brain and helped to heal much of the damaged tissue. For me, this has been one of the best ways of reversing the brain damage that has brought on aging. In the next chapter, we will discuss in detail how to keep your brain primed for a robust 120 years of existence.

STEM CELLS AND THE FUTURE OF AGING

You have over 220 different types of cells in your body. When all these cells work in harmony, you will feel and look great. Aging or extending life depends on you having beautiful healthy cells that are sending out the proper signals and creating an environment where your body can thrive.

You have trillions of cells all working together, but each of these cells has a finite lifespan. In fact, every minute that you are sitting here, you lose over 300 million cells. They die, and their work is complete.

If your cells just kept dying, what would happen to you?

Well, you'd die. This slow death is happening this very moment. The good news is that you have *master* cells in your body called stem cells that replace cells when they die. If you have enough healthy stem cells, you will slow your aging process.

Stem cell therapy is a newer medicine, and the more that I investigate it, the more fascinated and excited I become about the future because this is the foundational piece for creating longer and healthier life. Everything we talk about in this book will show you how to cultivate better stem cell proliferation and growth. I've also written a book called, *The Stem Cell Breakthrough: Reversing Pain and Chronic Disease and Getting Back to the Life You Love*. This book will give you a more in-depth perspective on this fascinating area of health. You can find it on Amazon or feel free to email me at info@gowellness.com, and I will send you a free digital copy.

For those of you who are looking for the regenerative properties of stem cells, there is a simple resource center called Stem Cell Health Centers that I have founded to create a network of the top physicians in the country using stem cell therapy. (stemcellhealthcenters.com) We have studies, articles, and rich content as well as practitioners whom you can connect with in your area.

> *WOW! This is the BEST DECISION WE MADE. My knees are better than ever before. I honestly can't remember my knees feeling this good. This is a MIRACLE. May GOD bless you ALL for what you are doing for humanity; this is way better than the bone marrow stem cells I had three years ago.*
>
> ~ John and Alison

300 Million Cells Die Every Minute

The key to restoring great function in your body and being able to adequately think, learn, and have a fun time with your physical body is to have continual expression of healthy cells. As you age, the number of stem cells decline as does the health of the stem cells.

Ever noticed how quickly kids heal?

Research performed by Neil Riordan, PhD shows that if you take a single newborn stem cell and grow it in a petri dish, you will find that after thirty days, this single stem cell becomes *one billion cells.*[1] This phenomenal growth means that it is exponentially growing—every twenty-four hours this one cell doubles in number. If you take a cell from a thirty-five-year old and put it in a petri dish, this stem cell will double only every forty-eight hours, so it is half as vibrant. And, by the end of thirty days, you will only have 32,000 stem cells—far different than newborn stem cell growth. If you place a single stem cell from a sixty-five-year old in a petri dish and grow it, after thirty days that person will only have 200 cells because their cellular doubling only happens every sixty hours.

As we age, we lose our stem cell healing potential. Not only do we lose the stem cells in our bodies, but our stem cells are as old as we are. What I have explored is how to put stem cells into my body that will be young, robust, and differentiate in a healthy way. So far, what I have found are the stem cells from amniotic birth tissue or perinatal tissue.

Perinatal stems cells can differentiate and become the different tissue structures needed after your body lost them in the aging and degenerative process. What these tissue allographs also do is hone-in on sites of inflammation and balance immune responses. They also help with blood vessel growth, reduce scarring, and repair and regenerate tissues.

---

1   Rogan, Joe. "#1066 – Mel Gibson & Dr. Neil Riordon." *The Joe Rogan Experience.* January 18, 2018. player.fm/series/the-joe-rogan-experience-142216/1066-mel-gibson-dr-neil-riordan

This is one of the novel sources of safe, healthy application of stem cell therapy.

Increase Stem Cells, Increase Small Intestine Health, and Decrease Aging

Do you ever feel older than your age?

There isn't much that's worse than waking up feeling like the Tin Man from *The Wizard of Oz*. While there are several reasons why you can feel less than your best, I've found that more often than not, once your diet is on point, you will start to feel your age or better. Like it or not, there are certain foods and nutrients that stem cells need to grow.

Research has shown that the stem cells found in the villi of your small intestine are some of the most active and densely populated in your entire body. If you increase the health of your small intestine, you will increase your stem cell release rate and increase your health. When you eat foods like sugar, gluten, or even casein—casein is a protein found in dairy—they deplete the proliferation of stems cells in your small intestine. Conversely, eating a time-restricted, low inflammation, high nutrient-based diet, has been shown to increase your stem cell release rate.

Do you feel like you need something sweet after meals?

The best solution that I can provide is installing a simple shock collar and camera on your body. It's simple; you reach for sugar; the camera notifies us; we shock you. We can program it for a variety of foods. Not a big deal, we've got your back. I'm joking! Actually, for some of you, this would be an effective solution, just not totally humane. Check out my book, *Your Health Transformation,* to dive into the ocean of nutrition and lifestyle, or call me up for a shock collar installation.

Your Long or Short-Lived Life

At the end of the day, your health independence is up to you. We are within striking distance of ending certain types of chronic pain and ending certain chronic diseases. Once these problems are solved, we can get on with the enjoyment of living. You have enough horsepower to stick this one out. Stay in the game; we need you.

I don't want you to look back twenty years from now wishing you would have done more to set yourself up to live well beyond your expected lifespan. Forget the bucket list.

Why retire when you've got nothing but wisdom, vitality, and value to give to the world?

Don't you want to see who wins the next Grammy award or national championship?

What about your kids and grandkids?

The choice to move towards health independence is a daily choice. It's a choice that will bring you the ultimate freedom that you are looking for. Investing in your health now will pay massive future dividends. Your investment now gives you a far more predictable outcome than was previously available. We've already seen a massive increase in lifespan, and it's only going to keep improving.

Now that you are fired up and ready to play a bigger, better game, you may be wondering: *What about my genetics?* Yep, we've got a handle on that. Or, *How about my hormones and immune health?* Once again, yes, we've got the tools to resolve your issues. *But, Regan, what about the arthritis and loss of cartilage?* No problem, we've got solutions. You've almost made it through Chapter One, and all these issues will be addressed as you read on.

I want to share my deep appreciation with you for joining me in the cause to end pain and chronic disease for one million people by 2025. I've seen too many amazing people die far too young, and I don't want to see that happen to any of you. You mean the world to me, and together we can extend living in the most meaningful ways.

What are three things that you can do today to improve your health by just 1 percent?

What are three things you can *stop* doing to improve your health by 1 percent today?

CHAPTER TWO

Your Healthy, Rejuvenated Brain

WHAT YOUR BRAIN NEEDS MOST

Your brain is arguably the most important organ in your body. It consumes 20 percent of our energy when we are awake and 25 percent of the electrical energy in our body when we are asleep. A healthy brain leads to a healthy body.

If there was a secret way to improve your brain performance 10 percent, would you do it?

One of the most important aspects of having health independence and extending your life is to have a healthy brain. There is no reason to live beyond eighty or ninety or even one hundred, if your brain goes to sleep on you. My goal is to put you in the driver's seat and give you the tools so that you can understand how to expand your brain's capacity because most of us have enormous potential in our brain that rarely gets captured. We discovered that brains are incredibly diverse and that they are considered *plastic*, which means our brains have the ability to *regenerate*.

Imagine that you are 120. You pick up a book, read it, and retain the knowledge. You can learn in whatever way you like; perhaps you are watching a movie, or you are on the internet—or, doing whatever forms of learning we will be doing in the future, and your brain is actively collecting knowledge. Not only are you a great student who learns quickly, but you can get up and exercise. You can walk.

How do you want your brain to function now?

What about three years from now?

I see so many elderly people who shuffle when they walk because their brains do not work well enough for their motor control to be engaged. Don't walk like you are old! Walk with dignity and your brain will follow suit. Part of having a healthy brain is also having a healthy physical body that allows you to move. This chapter is going to introduce you to some brand-new breakthroughs for a healthy 120-year-old brain.

Your Brains Need Fascinating and Challenging Things

Have you noticed how quickly your brain can take you down a path of destruction where you feel defeated in life?

Your brain is complex, and it can either point us in an unhealthy direction, or in a direction that allows you to thrive and experience life in a happy, meaningful way. We fill in the reality gaps with disturbing conclusions, most of which never come true. Trust me, I do it all the time! So, how we can avoid this is by *de-cluttering*.

Your brain likes an environment that is consistent and predictable. De-cluttering your environment can be a great place to begin. This will allow you to feel safe enough to explore new ideas and take on bigger risks that are potentially more rewarding.

What things can you get rid of?

What clothes haven't you worn in the last six months?

Get rid of them! You will soon realize that what you own actually owns you.

Now that you have gotten your environment cleared out, prepare your brain for new adventures with traveling. One reason I absolutely love travel is that my brain loves the challenge of planning a great trip and loves to absorb other cultures and experience life in new ways. I like to travel for pleasure at least every three months. I have found that it keeps me vibrant and full of gratitude for my amazing life. I can't think of a better place to live, but leaving my comfortable environment allows me to appreciate my community and life even more.

Where do you want to travel?

Get it on the calendar!

Learning, Emotions, And Purpose: Hardware Versus Software

How many times have you taken a class and tried to study a subject that was not of interest to you?

Think about the emotions that came up—the frustration. For many of us, the reason we are not interested in certain subjects is because of our brain's hardware, it has *nothing* to do with how smart or lazy you are.

I remember studying calculus in college and was not motivated by the subject at all. And fortunately, I had a great professor who created an environment where I could learn enough to pull out a B in the class. I just wanted the grade, but even with a world-class professor, I never wanted to study calculus again.

Contrast that with biology, which is incredibly fascinating to me, or philosophy or technology—these are fascinating subjects that motivate me to learn. You can have the calculus. Find a subject or two and dive deep. If you are reading this book, then my guess is that you enjoy learning about health. Me too. I am motivated to learn new things about brain health because I know I can inspire and enlighten thousands of people by helping them develop a healthier brain.

There is an emotional aspect that either accelerates or stunts learning. Engage in subjects that interest you, seek out mentors in those fields, take online courses, or enroll in local classes. The first step in creating a healthy brain is figuring out what you are fascinated by. And then, use the emotional energy to propel yourself forward to learn new things. As you are learning new things, the purpose of why you are studying it will bring more *meaning* to your life. The more knowledge you have, the more you can converse and connect with a variety of people.

Your brain has a set of hardware similar to your computer. But, the interesting thing about the brain is there are pieces of software, almost like having an app on your smart phone. These *apps* help you access much more data and intelligence than you could without these apps. The software in the brain is all the things that you are learning and skills you are gaining that enhance the ability for your brain to perform.

So, the hardware is there. And, the beautiful thing is we can always add software to enhance our intelligence, emotional experience, and meaning in our lives.

Alzheimer's Disease

Alzheimer's disease is quickly moving up as a leading disease in America, bypassing diabetes and heart disease in prevalence in people over the age of eighty.

One of the most tragic experiences of my life was watching my grandmother's brain health deteriorate with Alzheimer's disease. She was the most capable, responsive, energetic woman. She was an entrepreneur and a phenomenal grandmother, mother, and inspiration to all of us. Alzheimer's created a scenario where her brain was clouded with confusion.

My grandmother started sending me multiple birthday cards every month, and then she would call me by my cousin's name when we would meet in person. Her condition worsened to the point where the last memories I have of my grandmother are of her in a nursing home, full of paranoia and confusion. It was devastating to witness the destructive nature of this disease.

If you want to avoid conditions like Alzheimer's, which is now being called *type 3 diabetes,* you must control your glycemic variability. This means watching not only what you eat, but also when you eat.

Nutrition Simplified With Timed Eating

Research is showing us that it is not only what you eat that makes a difference in your health, but also *when* you eat. Give yourself a minimum of twelve hours per day when you are *not* eating anything at all, and you will have dramatic improvements in your health and blood sugar.

Get your healthy fats in the morning like:

- Avocado
- Coconut cream
- Wild caught fish
- Ghee
- Free-range organic eggs
- Colostrum
- Coconut yogurt

Add vegetables to the healthy fats like:

- Arugula
- Spinach
- Steamed kale
- Leafy greens
- Pea shoots
- Sprouted broccoli

Avoid fruits, carbohydrates, and meats in the morning. Repeat at lunchtime, and then add in healthy proteins and carbohydrates at dinner.

SIMPLE SOLUTIONS FOR GREAT BRAIN HEALTH

I found that the daily path to brain health is as simple as:

- Viewing your brain as a muscle
- Using your intellectual capabilities
- Connecting with your emotions

- Exercising, such as pushups to keep your upper body strong and squats to have fit legs
- Focusing your brain with mental exercises

It does not need to be complex. Cultivate a lifestyle and environment that help your brain—that is the simple secret. There are things that you can do that are certainly more complex, especially if you have had a concussion, or you have a neuro degenerative disease like Parkinson's, Alzheimer's, multiple sclerosis, or have had a stroke. These diseases will require a little more complexity, but it is as simple as getting the right foods in your diet and exercising on a regular basis. Then, do the things that energize you from a learning perspective while cultivating the right relationships and emotions to expand your capacity to have greater brain health.

Staying in the Moment

Think about what the word *deep-learning* means. One of my teachers, Dr. Chieko Maekawa, PhD, Lac, encouraged me to have a cotton-ball brain. I always thought that was kind of a funny Japanese thing, and it took me nearly ten years to understand the concept.

I read the book, *Zen Mind, Beginner's Mind*, by Shunryu Suzuki, and it helped open me up to what it means to have a *beginner's mind*. The beginner's mind has a cotton ball brain, and this means having the ability to stay so present in the moment that you can take in new things.

Most of us are so distracted by the problems in our day to day life or the shiny object on Facebook that we fail to learn the most important life lessons. If you find time every day where you have no distractions—where you have 100 percent presence—then you will learn new things much faster, and you will love it.

Being present in the moment becomes your meditation, which means you simply focus on one thing at a time. Focus on your breathing; that's meditation. Focus on your writing; that's meditation. It is how our brains connect with our bodies.

Interestingly, if you were to do a brain scan on someone who meditates often, you would find that their brain is far more active than people who do not meditate. And, in people who are meditating often, the brain actually has more neuro pathways that are active. The brain of someone who is meditating has more neuro activity than with someone who is distracted. When we are distracted, we create a whirlwind in our brains.

Right now, pause and take five deep breaths. Count five seconds on the inhale, pause, and five seconds for the exhale. Notice what it does to your brain. And, notice how much easier it is to read this book after you have done this simple exercise.

FITNESS, LEARNING, SLEEP, AND FUN

There is a molecule in your brain that has been extensively researched called *brain-derived neurotropic factor* (BDNF). One of the theories around having and maintaining a healthy brain—even up until you are 120 years old—is by maintaining adequate levels of brain-derived neurotropic factors.

How can you increase your BDNF?

There are at least four ways to accomplish this:

1. **Fitness**: Have the right exercise programs. Fitness is not just for the physical body. There are studies that prove that the more people exercise, the quicker they learn and the healthier their brain is. Remember, the brain requires a lot of your energy. And, the brain cannot receive energy if you are not physically fit. Block out at least an hour a day for exercise.

2. **Learning**: Learning habits are the second way to increase your BDNF. Find a quiet, peaceful, and creative place to devote an hour to learning and study without disruptions. Spend time reflecting on your life, your goals, and your relationships and determine where you can improve. Then, set up your daily action plan around your intentions. Afterwards, study what fascinates you most and really get your creative juices flowing.

3. **Sleep**: The better you sleep, the better your brain can organize. Did you know you can go longer without food than you can do without sleep? People have lived up to sixty days without food. With sleep deprivation, the record is only about two weeks. So, one of the most important things you can do is practice good sleep hygiene. This means no screens an hour before you go to bed. And, it also means that we need to have a dark and quiet sleep environment.

4. **Fun**: The final thing that helps kickstart a healthy brain is having fun. A study published in the journal, *Neuropsychopharmacology*, showed that being in a state of exploration—new, fun, and novel things—kick-starts more of the BDNF that our brains love in contrast to behaviors of withdrawal and avoidance.[2] Nothing is as refreshing as a good laugh and intense enjoyment. When you have fun, your brain will light up. And, this will affect everyone around you. Fun is good for all of us.

WHAT ABOUT MY ADDICTED BRAIN?

Every human—you and me—will have trauma in their brain because we all have emotions, and we have all experienced

---

2   *Cerebellar BDNF Promotes Exploration and Seeking for Novelty.* Neuropsycholopharmacology. 2018 May 21. Published online Feb 17. Doi:10.1093/ijnp/pyy015

adversity and setbacks in our life. Sometimes, these setbacks create addiction. One similarity behind all addiction is *brain inflammation.*

According to the American Society of Addiction Medicine, "Addiction is a primary, chronic disease of brain reward, motivation, memory and related circuitry." (asam.org)

According to an article in New Atlas, *How Stem Cell Therapy Could be a Future Cure for Alcoholism,* "Recent research has indicated that chronic use of addictive drugs, including alcohol, cocaine, and opiates, is associated with an increase in neuroinflammation. Other studies, in both humans and rats, have also suggested that pro-inflammatory conditions in the brain can increase voluntary alcohol consumption."[3]

A study published in *Alcohol and Alcoholism* by a team of researchers from the University of Chile found that stem cell infusions into high-alcohol intake bred rats resulted in the animals dramatically reducing alcohol consumption. Researchers found that after the stem cell treatments, the rats that historically chose the equivalent of a pint of vodka per day, were now drinking amounts typical of a social drinker.[4]

At my East West Health clinics, we have also seen dramatic recoveries with the patients who have undergone stem cell

---

3   Haridy, Rich. How stem cell therapy could be a future cure for alcoholism. New Atlas. March 22, 2018. newatlas.com/stem-cell-alcohol-addiction-treatment/53918/
4   Alcohol and Alcoholism. Volume 52, Issue 1. January 1, 2017.

therapy for their addictions. One of my patients who has been in and out of rehab for alcoholism for nearly twenty-five years received stem cell treatments, and now has not had a single desire for a drink since she had the treatment nearly one year ago. We have seen this pattern duplicated time and time again, but we also make sure that our patients have the necessary support structures around them and work with their psychologists and attend their AA meetings.

Realizing that your brain can heal when the inflammation is removed and the damaged brain cells are replaced with new stem cells is ground breaking. We will see more and more individuals finding relief with this novel treatment. Stem cell treatments have the potential to grow a brand-new life and give you a brand-new perspective and energy—even if you've failed with other treatments for addiction. It is a first line of therapy for anyone struggling with any type of addiction.

Understanding Our Brains

Our brains are complex, and if you look at it from an evolutionary perspective, our bodies had to sacrifice something in order to have a large brain. What we had to sacrifice was a long digestive track. Our digestive track is relatively small and short. Historically, we had to learn how to feed our brains because our brains are energy hungry machines.

One of the ways that we have done this is by having the ability to cook our foods. If we look at the differences in other primates, one is that they are not cooking their food. They only have the ability to eat a few varieties of food. In cooking our food, we enjoy greater diversity in what we can eat. This diversity creates an environment where we have a variety of bacteria, and these bacteria directly influence our brain's functions. Surprisingly, we have more nerves endings in our intestines than we do in our entire spinal cord. Bacteria release chemicals and create precursors for our brain to make neurotransmitters.

If you want to have a healthier brain, make sure you are getting a diversity of foods into your body. We use a test called Viome to measure the diversity of bacteria. I was fortunate enough to spend some time with Naveen Jain, the founder of Viome, and even had Naveen on my podcast to speak about Viome. He believes he can help create a world that is free from disease by focusing on the bacteria in the gut. The science his team uses with Viome is some of the most innovative available. We do this testing because the bacteria in your gut are going to influence the neurotransmitters that your brain needs to function at its ideal level.

From an evolutionary perspective, our brains have exploded in knowledge, understanding, and in growth. Our brains are almost twice the size of other primates. Therefore, we *must* receive better nutrition for our brains. We also have a greater ability to simplify the amount of time we eat. Humans chew food for about an hour a day, on average. I can think of a few days where I've outdone that number. Other apes and primates spend up to five hours a day chewing. One of the beautiful things about a smaller digestive system is that we absorb nutrients quicker. This speed allows us to feed our healthy brains.

Your Bigger and Better Future Brain

How many phone numbers do you remember?

Is that number fewer than the phone numbers that you remembered before you had a cell phone?

When I was a kid, I remembered everyone's phone number, and I would see it in my brain.

I remember I would like to challenge people, saying, "Tell me your phone number. Okay, ask me in thirty minutes if I still remember it."

I could remember phone numbers because I had a way of accessing and plugging in that information into the hardware of my brain. Now, we all have a cell phone. This cell phone is essentially an extension of our brain. So, as we look to the future we ask: *Well, what is going to change ten or twenty years from now because we are all on this exponential curve where technology is becoming faster, better, cheaper, and smaller than it has ever been before?*

We can use this technology to enhance the health of our brain or diminish it. The more we can prepare for bigger opportunities with technology, the better we are going to live.

My goal would be to make sure that future technology limits our exposure to electrical magnetic fields (EMFs) as they are destructive to your brain. We need to make sure that we have firewalls that can protect our brain from the technology. We also need to use technology to create a bigger, funnier, and more creative brain. This will be a fascinating part of the future.

CHAPTER THREE

Ending Pain and Extending Life with Stem Cells

My hip has severe osteoarthritis. I could either get a replacement or do stem cells. I chose stem cells. The staff is wonderful to work with, and I love the plan that I'm following. My health and pain improved significantly in the first week. I've had my injection and continue to improve. I recommend anyone wanting to seek relief and willing to follow a health plan to see East West Health!

~ Chris M

HOW TO MAKE PAIN AND CHRONIC DISEASE OPTIONAL

Ending pain and chronic disease is my quest because, just like you, I have struggled to find real answers to pain. I was riddled with pain in my early twenties, and most mornings I would wonder how I could possibly make it through the day.

Not only was my body in pain, but I had a hard time with my mind. Pain and chronic disease take away the joy of life, which makes them the most expensive thing we can have in life because they limit our choices.

How motivated are you to go for a hike when you can barely walk?

If you have ever experienced pain, think about what your energy reserves were like. Then, think about your relationships, your ability to enjoy life, and your ability to work. All these were diminished because of the pain and suffering that you were experiencing.

How do we treat pain?

We still rely on surgery and opiates, and yes, we are in an opiate crisis. Pain is exhausting. It robs your brain of energy, and research shows that it can age our brain ten to twenty years.

Think about: what is the cost of pain?

Imagine if we could live in a world where chronic disease was optional. Where we could use technology to reverse it. Imagine that you have an autoimmune disease like Hashimoto's, MS, ALS, or Parkinson's, like many of my patients have. Or, imagine you could take away your rheumatoid arthritis—like we have already helped many patients do.

But, what's wrong with medication?

Yes, medications can be lifesaving, but what are they treating?

Are you or someone you know on five or more medications?

The term for this is polypharmacy syndrome. A seventy-seven-year-old patient named Don came into the clinic for help with his rheumatoid arthritis. In his medical intake, we discovered he was on sixteen medications. His kidneys and liver were shutting down, presumably, from polypharmacy complications. Don realized that he had a choice: he could take his health into his own hands and do something different about his health, or he could continue on the medication downward spiral. Within forty-five days of his stem cell treatment, Don was able to get off the majority of his medications. Better yet, Don is now walking again, hunting, has lost sixty-seven pounds, and is free from pain.

Now, imagine the difference that you could make in someone's life if we could end chronic disease. If we could end pain, then not only would we stop the opiate epidemic that we have in our country, but we would also have the capabilities to help people find the true cause of their pain. When we resolve pain, it is not only on a physical level but also on an emotional level. Most of our patients who have had chronic pain also have emotional issues that need to be addressed.

The CDC estimates that nearly 70 percent of diseases are chronic, lifestyle driven diseases that can be reversed.

What are we doing about it?

Why are we in a health crisis when we have access to more information than Bill Clinton had when he was president, but still we are getting sicker, fatter, and more depressed?

While it is great to have access to endless information, we don't realize that we have equal access to misinformation that has misled us for decades. This misinformation is led by profit-driven industries that want you to be a patient for life. The dictionary.com "2018 Word of the Year" was *misinformation,* and I think now more than ever we need to be correctly informed about non-drug and non-surgical options to end pain and chronic disease.

My goal in talking about the purpose of ending pain and chronic disease is to give people the realization that there is a *solution.* You do not have to rely on expensive drugs and risky surgeries to end your pain and chronic disease. What you need to start focusing on is the abundance of health that exists inside your body. It starts with a mindset shift and a focus off the symptoms and onto the root cause of what is contributing to your pain and chronic disease. This is when you can really have a transformation in your health.

Where is your pain?

What are the steps you will take to alleviate it?

> *Total knee replacement was eminent, but I decided to get stem cell therapy at East West Health over six*

months ago. I can now climb stairs again without any problem, and I am playing golf again and going about my normal life again. I am very satisfied with the results I got and would recommend East West Health to anyone out there experiencing pain and lack of mobility. I would do it again tomorrow. Thank you, East West Staff.

~ Gary D

Ending Pain With Stem Cell Therapy

I had two choices: I could hit a tree or hit a skier. I love trees, so I collided with the skier at 40 mph. Fortunately, the skier was just fine, but I completely wrecked my shoulder in what turned out to be my worst snowboarding accident ever.

The imaging showed I had torn my rotator cuff, my labrum was damaged, and my scapula was fractured all but a half of an inch. The orthopedic doctor recommended surgery because she didn't know much about stem cells. So, after months of research, I decided to try stem cell therapy from perinatal tissue, not from my own body.

Within three days after the stem cell therapy on my injured shoulder, the pain decreased substantially. By ninety days after stem cells, I was at least 80 percent better. Six months later, my shoulder was just as strong as it was before my accident. I am incredibly happy to say that I am *still pain free* after a single injection.

Pain can bring out the worst in us. It creates an environment where we are not excited about life. I investigated some of the best ways of ending pain and chose to practice acupuncture. Acupuncture is a great option for many conditions, but for chronic pain, nothing has yielded reproducible results like stem cells.

Stem cells shut down inflammation and repair and regenerate tissue. They prevent premature cell death and reduce scar tissue. This next-gen treatment is one of the most phenomenal breakthroughs that I have seen. If you are suffering with chronic pain, your wait is over. Come see us at East West Health or find a practitioner in your area who has been trained by my team at East West Health.

> *I was two days away from shoulder surgery and couldn't lift my arm from my side and got stem cells and have loved them! No surgery and easy recovery!*
> ~ Donna S

The Solutions for Longevity Exist

The solutions for longevity are many. If you read the book, *The Blue Zones,* by Dan Buettner, you will find that there are multiple studies on the super centenarians, or people who have lived beyond 110 years (National Geographic Society, 2010). But, you will see that they all vary.

One person will say, "It is because I drank red wine every day and I smoke a cigarette."

The other person will say, "It is because I did not drink wine and I did not smoke."

Currently, the oldest living person is 122, but how many of you would want to live to be that age?

Exactly! No one does unless they are healthy. Premature morbidity is living in a diseased state. I have more and more patients coming to see me in their thirties who have had heart attacks. They have diabetes and they're obese. We must make healthy living a daily pursuit, otherwise why even try to extend our lives?

There really is no consistent pattern to show how super centenarians get to where they are. But, what we do know is that longevity and confronting age is something that is within striking distance. We have learned through cellular health and a process called *autophagy* that we can regenerate the cells in our body. Autophagy stems from two Greek words: *auto* means self, and *phagy* means to eat. So, autophagy means you are eating the cells that are no longer healthy in your body.

Practice activities that trigger autophagy in your body:

- Time restrictive eating
- Fasting
- Exercise
- Saunas
- Cold exposure

When autophagy kicks in, it allows your cells to repair themselves. You will also have better stem cell health and circulation. These two factors will allow you to distribute nutrients through every cell, organ, and tissue structure in your entire body. Triggering the autophagy process in your body is one of the primary breakthroughs for expanding your age and increasing longevity.

One of *Your Healthy Self* goals is to increase autophagy and decrease the chances of cells going into senescence, which is when cells die off entirely. Then, you can receive stem cell infusions from perinatal tissue—every six months to a year— to enhance your overall ability to age gracefully and extend your youthfulness as long as possible. I want you to live to age 150.

A study published in the Journal of Gerontology was the first ever human study to show that stem cells can reverse the frailty of elderly patients with "remarkable improvements in physical performance measures and inflammatory biomarkers."[5] The average age of the patients was seventy-five. The objective measure of inflammation, the cell-signaling protein TNF-alpha, falls after an infusion of mesenchymal stem cells. In both animals and people, the C-reactive protein level remains

---

5   Tompkins, BA, et al. "Allogeneic Mesenchymal Stem Cells Ameliorate Aging Frailty: A Phase II Randomized, Double-Blind, Placebo-Controlled Clinical Trial." *The Journals of Gerontology*. Series A, Volume 72, Issue 11. 12 October 2017, PP 1513-1522. Doi: 10.1093/gerona/glx137

lower for six to twelve months. The cells also appear to be safe. University of Miami cardiologist Joshua Hare says, "working in medicine thirty years, I've never seen anything this well tolerated."

CREATING AN ABUNDANCE OF HEALTH

The moment you *stop* creating health, you *start* creating sickness. This starts with what you put into your mouth, with the thoughts you think, and with the way you move your body. All health starts with having appreciation for the life that you have. Once you start fostering appreciation, then you start seeing innovative pathways and new modes of healing.

One of my patients, we will call her Sally, has spent decades of her life looking for solutions for her fibromyalgia. She raised five kids over the course of about twenty-five years, with many of her days stuck in bed because she was so sick. But, she was someone who never quit thinking that her body could heal, and she worked with the best doctors and healers that existed. The fact that she never gave up was amazing because she was able to get herself healthy and out of bed. Sally was diligent in receiving acupuncture treatments and stem cell therapy, and she would not have had that opportunity if she did not believe that health was *abundant*—she only had to find it.

Malfunctions and Disease Occur Long Before the Symptoms

Many of us are walking around with conditions like diabetes and heart disease, and we have no idea that it even exists.

David was incredibly fit and active and a remarkably successful venture capitalist. He was working twelve-hour days, and then he would rush to the gym and push himself beyond healthy levels. He was not eating as well as he could, but he had extremely low body fat. David ended up having a stroke.

The stroke damaged part of David's brain. It damaged his brain to the point where he lost coordination and the ability to speak and articulate. He could not move his facial nerves. What this event showed David is that malfunctions can go undetected until eventually something big happens.

David had lab tests run and everything was looking great. His doctors told him: *you are the picture of health*. But, his stroke was a wake-up call because he realized there were deeper issues not being addressed. He decided to take an unusual route to treat his stroke and restore his health by receiving intranasal stem cells treatments at our clinic.

Not only have the intranasal stem cells treatments helped David regain his coordination and his movements, but his mental sharpness is back on track. He was also able to get treatments in parts of his spine and shoulder—which had been holding him back—as well as his right knee. And, through this novel treatment, he has been able to restore most of his health. I am happy to say that David has also started meditating.

Wanting an Incredible Life Leads to an Abundance of Health

I found that people rarely allow themselves to create an incredible life. Most people expect the worst out of life and constantly live life on their heels. But, what I learned from my mentors, Dan Sullivan and Dr. Chieko Maekawa, is that knowing what you want in life is one of the most precious gifts you can give yourself. Yet, few people know what they want in life, and very few people have goals.

I am always telling my kids, "Know what you want and be firm on what you want. You are not always going to get what you want, from the material perspective, but if you know what you want, then it creates this ability to start looking at life as more abundant."

You will start to multiply the transformations that are possible just by wanting an incredible life. The more life you want to have—the more life you want to live—the more risks you may need to take.

I went on a helicopter skiing trip in British Columbia recently, and it was one of the most invigorating, enriching experiences of my life. I experienced snowboarding in terrain that was very intimidating. My friend Rudy and my brother Cade made the experience ten times better. Their enthusiasm is always contagious, and I loved being out there with two of my favorite people on the planet. Without health and friendship, I would have missed out on one of the most invigorating experiences of my life.

> *After struggling for many years—really my entire life—with misdiagnosed and overwhelming digestive issues, I was recommended to East West Health by a friend of my mother's. In the beginning, I was hesitant due to the money necessary to invest in the program, but after six months—which flexibly turned into a year—I would have spent that and more to receive the care I did from this facility.*
>
> ~ Lauren E

CULTIVATING ABUNDANT HEALTH REQUIRES CULTIVATING AMAZING RELATIONSHIPS

I love the quote that says: *You are the five people that you associate with the most.*

I think there is another part of the quote that says: *You are also the five books that you read the most.*

When focusing on abundant health, one of the influential pieces will be the people you spend time with. Think about the person that you did not like spending a lot of time with as a child. Maybe, there was someone in school who was a bully, or somebody who just did not make you feel good. Or, perhaps you had a manipulative mother, father, or sibling. Think about those people who could draw out all your energy. We have all experienced a conversation with someone who left us completely exhausted. That is not a relationship I want.

I want relationships that leave me feeling happy. My grandfather, Reo Archibald, was one of those individuals in my life who always made me feel good about myself. When we would be working on the farm, we would wake up early and work all day until sundown. All throughout the day my grandfather would complement me. He would tell me I was a toiler, a good worker.

My grandfather served in WWII and did not talk about it until the end of his life, but he always had something nice to say. Even though he was in incredible pain at certain times, people could depend on my grandfather to give them great advice and help them feel amazing about themselves. Professionally, he created novel curriculum for students with learning disabilities and special needs. He gave up a prestigious role as a principal at one of the major school districts in Idaho so he could do this.

I think about my grandfather often, and I think about abundance of health that he has created in me just from the love and the acceptance that he has always shown me throughout my life. Now, I hope to provide that same love and acceptance to people whom I meet. From my grandfather, I learned that life is about love and connection. It is not about having the right answers or impressing others; it is about appreciating what you have and being clear on what you want.

We All Need Mentors

One of my first mentors in health was Dr. Bauman at the University of Utah. He taught several interesting courses, some physiology courses, but also a course on the history of medicine. Dr. Bauman was somebody who thought outside the conventional box. He was in his late eighties and still teaching, still passionate. He was maybe five foot one, just a small guy, but he spoke as if he were a giant.

The energy Dr. Bauman carried radiated. He led me down a path to look at health through a new lens. I had always, through my own illnesses, had a desire to learn how to get my body more physically fit by eating the right foods. Dr. Bauman helped me choose a path out of conventional medical school and into an integrated medical school in Hawaii, which is where I did my training.

While I was in Hawaii, I was able to meet my next mentor, Dr. Chieko Maekawa. She taught me the way to be present with my patients and to diagnose them. Dr. Maekawa taught me the way to palpate and look beyond the imaging on an X-ray or MRI, so I could truly see the patterns of malfunction in somebody's body long before an image or a lab test could give the diagnosis. To end pain and chronic disease, we all need mentors who can point us in the right direction.

People often ask me: *Regan, are you mentoring others?*

Absolutely. This book, my training programs, and patient work are all ways I mentor. I also mentor about 100 healthcare providers in a group I founded called Go Wellness.

Do you have a mentor?

If you do, what do you like about your mentor?

Does your mentor help push you and give you guidance on a proper path to take?

One of the biggest challenges we are faced with as a society is we do not have mentors doing deep, deep work with us.

Dr. Maekawa would say, "The deeper you dig your well, the purer the water would be at the bottom of the well."

We all need mentors. We need mentors for all the major aspects of our lives.

My challenge to you right now is: *Who is your mentor? Are they pushing you in the direction you need to go?*

Nobody Can Do It Alone

Often, we get an idea in our head that we must do everything ourselves. This is simply not true. Once you start to appreciate and feel a deep sense of gratitude for the people around you, then you start to cooperate with them. When it comes to finding your path, don't think of what you must do, think about who can help you reach the goal you are trying to achieve.

One of the quotes that I like is by William Osler, "A physician who treats himself has a fool for a patient."

This is a quote that I have learned from because sometimes, I have wanted to do it alone, and that is when I have had my worst health.

Who can you reach out to today for guidance?

Your Health Team

Creating a team is fun. And, if you think about creating a health team around you, you are going to be the captain of this team.

A team captain is always receiving feedback, right?

They want to know how all the players on the field are doing, how they are feeling, and what they are experiencing. Then, the captain can facilitate the overall game. You are the captain of your health, and it is ultimately in your hands. Your own personal health is up to you. I do not want you dependent on me, a medication, herb, supplement, or anyone else for your health. You can do this, but you need a team around you.

We cannot see the blind spots. You may think: *Oh, my doctor is very smart; she can figure this out for me.* But, your doctor has only one brain. It takes multiple brains to bring together what needs to happen to keep you healthy.

The next level of health can't be reached without having a team around you. Having a health team can help you differentiate all your lab data and show you how to do something meaningful with it. I believe that healthcare teams consisting of doctors, acupuncturists, and health coaches are your most valuable resource for long-term health.

> *I have been going to East West Health for about two and a half years now, and it has been a life changing experience. I work in the healthcare industry and had been unable to get any help from traditional medicine for the symptoms I was having. East West helped me to heal my gut, eliminate the aches and pains, eliminate my constant autoimmune flare ups, and brought back my energy.*
>
> *I would—and have—recommended them for anyone who has medical problems of any kind, especially if they haven't been able to find solutions. I am now learning how my body works and have the knowledge to make more and more of my own decisions about what my body needs. I know I can always come back to them if I get stuck again, and that kind of confidence is very freeing after decades of pain and suffering. It's like having an ace in my*

back pocket. Monthly maintenance visits will help me stay balanced. My future looks great, and I owe it all to East West Health.

~ Connie T

CHAPTER FOUR

Three Habits for Great Energy

This is a place to find ANSWERS, not band-aids to improve your health.

~ Mindi J.

ALIGNING WITH YOUR BODY'S CIRCADIAN RHYTHMS

Our bodies follow the universal patterns of light and darkness. In Chinese medicine, this concept is represented with yin and yang. It is a way of describing the natural rhythms of the earth and our body. The natural rhythm of our bodies is also called the circadian clock.

When your circadian rhythm is healthy, you will find you:

- Sleep better
- Are more alert during the day
- Experience better cardiovascular ability

- Experience greater muscle strength and reaction time
- Experience optimal liver function
- Experience appropriate release of insulin

If your circadian rhythm is disrupted, then you may have poor sleep quality, more depression, and mental health issues.

One of the keys to having amazing energy and feeling like your most vibrant, vital self is to *follow* the circadian rhythms. We live in an era where we can have the lights on for the entire day. We can go without sleep if we want. We can push the envelope when it comes to these healthy circadian rhythms, and many of us think that we can skip sleep and stay healthy.

The truth is, we can go longer without food than we can without sleep. Yet, most of us minimize the time that we spend in bed and don't really take a hard look at how and when we are eating. Most of us also don't look at the appropriate time to exercise. Improving your energy is best accomplished by following the circadian rhythms.

How are you doing with aligning your lifestyle with your environment?

Have you noticed how you feel when you are synchronized compared to when you are not?

A Good Night's Sleep

To get a good night sleep, go to bed at a set time at night and wake up at a set time in the morning. For example, my wife likes to be in bed by 9:00 p.m. and wake up at 4:40 a.m. almost every morning. I have often wondered why we need sleep, and there are multiple explanations. We do know, as I mentioned earlier, that we can go longer without food than we can go without sleep. It has been documented that people can go up to sixty days without eating. I do not recommend trying that, but with sleep you cannot go much more than a couple of weeks.

The best way to sleep like the king or queen you are is to start thinking about the ways that our bodies wake up. You have a powerful hormone called cortisol. Cortisol is secreted at the opposite time of melatonin. Melatonin is one of the most important hormones secreted by your pineal gland when it is time to sleep.

In the healthy body, cortisol is higher in the morning. Then, as the night starts to wind down, melatonin starts to kick in. Melatonin secretion starts right around nine o'clock. This hormone cycle also depends on the cycles of the sun. If it is winter, then the melatonin secretion may start a little sooner. If it is summer, it may start later.

The best way to get your body regulated is to follow a pattern of sleep. If you like to go to sleep around 9:30 p.m., start winding down around 8:30 p.m. This is a great time to grab a book. It is also a good time to avoid any blue lights. Look around at the lights in your house because many of us have these blue lights. If you can change those to amber colored lights, or even put on some blue-light-blocking glasses, that will help the melatonin secretion process.

Then, when it is time to go to bed, your body and your brain will be in a state where you can fall into a much deeper sleep. Ideally, you will sleep in a room that is below 70 degrees with nice air flow. Also, block out any kind of light that could come into your room or wear a sleep mask. You will sleep longer and have less stress because you are engaging your body in a process for good sleep. These are some of the ways that will help you wake up feeling amazingly refreshed and in harmony with your circadian clock.

Your Body's Internal Clocks

Internal clocks regulate your vital organs, muscles, and body chemistry by regulating three to six thousand gene expressions on a daily cycle. Nearly 25 percent of your genes are on a clock. So, it is important to follow these rhythms.

The environment around us, like the cycles of the sun and the moon, also regulates your internal clocks. At six in the morning, we have the sharpest rise in our blood pressure. Melatonin secretion stops right around 7:30 a.m. Your testosterone is the highest right around 9:00 a.m., which is one reason why our libido can be higher in the morning. Our levels of alertness are the highest around 10:00 a.m. Between then and 3:30 p.m. is a good time to be productive. This is when you can accomplish the most focused work of the day.

Your best coordination for the day is going to be right around 2:30 p.m., so it is a great time to attend a yoga class. And, your fastest reaction time is going to be around 3:30 p.m. Your cardiovascular efficiency and muscle strength will peak around 5:00 p.m. So, if you are going to be in a body building competition, make sure that you are on stage at five in the evening.

The highest rise in blood pressure is going to be around 6:30 p.m., and 7:00 p.m. is when we have the highest body temperature. Then, our bodies start to down-regulate, and by 9:00 p.m., when melatonin secretion starts, it is time to go to bed. Our bodies go through about four or five rem cycles in a health sleep pattern, and our deepest sleep usually happens around 2:00 a.m. Then, our body temperature drops to its lowest point at 4:30 a.m. And then we wake up at 6:00 a.m. and things move forward.

Bacteria in Your Gut Follow a Circadian Rhythm

One of the studies that was done on circadian rhythms was done on mice. They analyzed different bacteria inside the mice, looking at the activity of these bacteria at different times of the day. What they found was that certain species of bacteria are active at night and quiescent in the day. Then inversely, they found that there are certain bacteria that are much more active during the day and less active at night.

Studies from Dr. Satchin Panda's book, *The Circadian Code*, showed that mice on a twenty-four-hour feeding cycle ended up having more diabetes, obesity, and disease compared to the group of mice that only had access to food for an eight-hour eating window—even though their calories were the same. Over the course of four months, the mice that had access to food on the twenty-four-hour diet had 38 percent more fat than the mice that were on the eight-hour diet.[6]

The easiest way to have a healthy metabolism and gut is to go through periods of fasting every day. Give your day an eight-hour window when you are eating food. It is a great way to regulate the bacteria in your gut. You will also find that you have better fat burning potential, and many digestive issues will go away.

---

6   Panda, Satchin. The Circadian Code: Lose Weight, Supercharge Your Energy, and Transform Your Health from Morning to Midnight. New York: Crown Publishing, a division of Penguin Random House, 2018.

CHANGING YOUR LIFE WITH TIMED EATING

When You Eat is as Important as What You Eat

Timed eating is when you choose periods throughout the day to eat and to not eat. Hugh Jackman is a big advocate of timed eating, as are other body builders and experts in the fitness world like Ben Greenfield. With time restrictive eating, simply map out when you will be eating in a twenty-four-hour period and stick to it. Make the decision once, and then you won't get decision-making fatigue. I like eating between 10:00 a.m. and 6:00 p.m., like Hugh Jackman.

What times are you eating?

Can you condense that time frame?

It starts with the first thing that goes in your mouth in the morning, like coffee or tea. Some people would say that you are still fasting as long as you are not putting calories into your body, but I prefer to start the clock the moment I ingest anything but water. With timed eating, you do not want to put anything into your body during the fasting portion of the day that will wake up your liver and cause the metabolic cycle to start. The best thing you can do is drink lots of water with a pinch of sea salt. Salt does not require any metabolic activity from your body.

Timed eating is different than intermittent fasting because you give your digestive system a complete break. If you give your liver a complete break that means no vitamins, supplements, coffee, or tea until it's also time for food. Just water with a little bit of salt in it. And, pick a period—maybe it is between 12:00 p.m. and 8:00 p.m. or between 10:00 a.m. and 6:00 p.m.—but whatever time frame you choose, try to stick to it at least five days a week. In the studies from *The Circadian Code,* it has been found that time restrictive eating, even if you do it five days a week, will have benefits.[7] So, give it a try; it will make an amazing difference in your digestion, energy, and capabilities to burn fat as energy.

Far too often we become caught up in what foods to eat and how many calories, grams of protein, fats, and carbohydrates—but start simple when it comes to nutrition and focus on when you are eating as your first step. When you are thinking about when you are eating it can be one of the most empowering ways to live your life because you are not a slave to eating food day and night. When the dessert comes out or you are offered another drink, you are not going to do it because you have already made the decision that you are eating only within a certain time frame. I find it makes choices much easier.

---

7   Panda, Satchin. *The Circadian Code: Lose Weight, Supercharge Your Energy, and Transform Your Health from Morning to Midnight.* New York: Crown Publishing, a division of Penguin Random House, 2018.

Not Missing a Day of Exercise

As we age, we need more exercise to keep up with the loss of stem cell release rates. Now that you are out of pain and energized from the new habits you have picked up in *Your Healthy Self,* you are ready to exercise every single day. Please do not skip a day. I would not advocate doing a high intensity workout every single day of the week, but mix it up with swimming, running, and biking, along with more primal movement workouts like CrossFit or an Orange Theory Fitness workout.

I do best if I practice yoga at least one day per week. Then, I have three or four days when I am doing a mix of cardio work with high intensity weight training. And, I keep one to two days per week for more heavy lifting. I also snowboard and mountain bike as often as I can and still do workouts even when I am enjoying myself in the Park City mountains.

If you are concerned about injuring yourself, then work with a physical therapist or a trainer before you load up the weights. The book, *Body by Science,* by Dr. Doug McGuff and John Little, which instructs on the super slow method, is a great resource for how to grow muscle mass without injuring yourself (McGraw Hill, 2009). Tabata training is a fun, effective way to get started with high intensity as well. If you love to run, then reach out to Danny Dreyer for some helpful ways to run without hurting yourself with his ChiRunning system (chirunning.com).

I look at my exercise as a way of keeping not only my body healthy, but my brain as well. Exercise has been proven to be one of the best ways to increase brain-derived neurotropic factors—which improve cognition and mental acuity. Just this morning, I took Zoe, my fourteen-year-old daughter with me to an Orange Theory Fitness workout, and we both felt incredibly energized after the workout. That energy stayed with us.

Think about how good you feel when you are done with a workout. Keeping your body healthy and your joints limber will give you a huge accomplishment at least for the day. Focus on keeping proper form so that you can exercise until the day you die.

People often ask me: *Regan, when is the best time to exercise?*

It depends on the health of your adrenal glands. You can find out with a simple twenty-four-hour salivary test we can provide. Basically, whenever cortisol levels drop and are at their lowest point, that is a great time of day to exercise. Some of you will do better exercising at night because, as we know from circadian rhythms, you will have better cardiovascular endurance at this time. You also tend to have better strength at night. Look at what works with your schedule and follow it every single day, and you will feel amazing.

Fasting Encourages Healthy Stem Cell Growth

Fasting is one of the easiest ways to repair your digestive system and leaky gut. Your body has reservoirs of stem cells and these stem cells are quiescent unless there is a stress placed on our bodies. Once there is a stress, then our stem cells activate and can go to work repairing damaged tissues.

When you put yourself in a fasting state, stem cells will start to migrate from the small intestine. These CD34 stem cells will start homing in on the areas of your body that have been damaged. The other thing that happens when you fast is your body goes into autophagy. As you learned earlier in this book, autophagy is when the body actually starts feeding on itself. Your body will start to rid itself of the old debris so that the new stem cells can grow and repopulate the areas that have been damaged.

Your intestines are regrown every two to three days. We have a brand-new liver every three to five days, and a new brain every five to seven days. So, fasting is one of the ways that you can accomplish regeneration all the organs, tissues, and glands in your body. Give fasting a try. Even if you try intermittent fasting—or if you decide you want to branch out and do a five-day water fast—you will find it to be beneficial.

STARTING EVERY DAY WITH A MINDSET MORNING RITUAL

If you can set an intention for the day, then it is much easier to focus on the things that will really help you feel fulfilled and add meaning in your life. Our life is made up of a series of days, and if you can create one amazing day, then you could create an amazing life.

To create a mindset morning ritual, you will:

- State your intentions for the day.
- Focus on the things you are grateful for.
- Visualize how you will feel when you accomplish your daily goals.

A mindset morning is a way of tuning your brain to focus on the things you want to focus on. It tunes your brain to look at the positive; otherwise, our brains are hardwired to focus on negativity. That is why all the news stations are constantly pumping out negative stories. They know that it sells, and people will listen. But, starting your day with a morning mindset can be transformative.

A mindset morning is something that I believe in doing every single day. I find that the better my state of mind in the morning, the easier it is for me to sleep at night—even if I haven't been able to have the perfect day I wanted. If you would like to see my entire process, simply go to YouTube and type in: *Regan Archibald, Mindset Morning*.

Meditation, Affirmations, and Visualization

Meditation for me was quite intimidating. I remember my first meditation teacher was Genpo Roshi, the creator of The Big Mind Process (bigmind.org). He is a phenomenal teacher, but I remember I would sit and all I would think about was my sore back, my knees, my inflexibility, or my hip pain. Then, I would start thinking about the problems of the day—it was like taming a wild horse. It took time, but soon I found that I was able to sit for those thirty-minute sessions in silence.

The conversations that would come after these meditations were impactful and enlightening. As Genpo Roshi would take us through The Big Mind Process, I was able to uncover a lot of subconscious thoughts and energy. Once I was able to unstick that, then I was able to move into a much bigger understanding of my life.

Meditation can be accomplished by focusing on a word like love, happiness, or gratitude. Meditation can also be accomplished through intentional breathing. In Asia, they practice what is called Qi Gong or Tai Chi, and it is a form of meditation.

When I go for long runs, my mind moves into a state of meditation. I also do this if I am lifting weights, mountain biking, or snowboarding. There are multiple ways of looking at meditation, but the definition is "focusing on one thing at a time."

In addition to meditation, start adding visualizations and goals for your day. What you will experience is your body creating the reality for your day because you are visualizing it. Your brain lays out all the physical parts needed to make it a reality. You want your brain to be tuned in to the things that you are trying to accomplish—things that are positive and will help serve your life and the planet. So, as you start to do your meditations, you will also learn different affirmations that help you stay motivated and confident. One of the biggest gifts you can give yourself is starting each day and constantly migrating back to this meditative cycle.

All Progress Begins With Gratitude

It is easy to look at the world and focus on all the chaos around us to justify being angry at the way things are. In this pattern, we fall into a scarcity mentality where we tell ourselves: *There are not enough resources to go around. I don't have friends that I would like to have or the work environment I want. I don't have the ability to do what other people do because they have more opportunities than I do.*

One of the best ways to move out of this scarcity mindset—the belief that life is not enough and there are not enough resources to go around—is to start looking at all the amazing things that you have. My mentor, Dan Sullivan, taught me that the quickest way to shift from scarcity to abundance is gratitude. We cannot hold negativity and gratitude at the same time. Gratitude is the bridge that brings us into our more creative side of thinking and bridges our heart with our brain so we start experiencing life's fullness. Life is full of endless possibilities and endless potential, and gratitude is the only way you can start to see it.

Have you ever been mad at someone or had to confront a person whom you felt wronged you?

Before you meet with them, write down a handful of things that you like about them or what you are grateful for in them. You will find that all that negative energy just goes away. Then, you can have a real conversation with them and move past the negativity. I believe gratitude is the great energetic mover. It will get us out of any stagnant place we are in and help us see much bigger potential and possibility in life.

Focus on Goals, Obstacles, Opportunity, and Collaboration

If you are looking to chart out a long, healthy, meaningful life, then one of the best ways to do it is to always have something bigger you are working toward. Dan Sullivan has a twenty-five-year process where he visualizes into the future and sees what will keep him fascinated and motivated for the next twenty-five years. He sets up his life that way.

I think one of the most powerful things that you can do is have a big project that you are working on or a big goal you are trying to achieve. If you don't have one, then you will become bored and end up in trouble. Your key is to stay fascinated. The same applies to your health. Each day, do something that makes you just a little bit healthier than the day before. See if you can't enjoy your day just a tiny bit more and take just a little more care of yourself and the ones you love most.

Create an abundance mentality around constant health. Once this is done, you are not going to get sick because you are always on the lookout for new ways to attract better health. As you set these goals, you will see that the universe will start to provide all that you need to create much better health, brainpower, and an ability to learn and grow.

No matter what age you are, no matter how sick or ill you may be right now, think about how you can make tomorrow just a little bit healthier than yesterday. You will be amazed at the amount of resources and potential that will come your way. Once you start to realize the opportunities around you, you will find there are people who are actually where you want to be, and these people are whom you want to learn from.

Whom do you admire who is older than you and also healthy and fit? Reach out to them.

If you hang out with people who are sick and complaining about their health all the time, then that might be where you end up. So, look for people who have done what you want to do and become friends with them. Read their books, attend their trainings, do their programs, or hire them as a trainer.

These are the ways that collaboration can help you grow ten times faster than doing it on your own.

CHAPTER FIVE

Pathway to Health Independence

HEALTH INDEPENDENCE IS EASY; HEALTH DEPENDENCE IS HARD

The biggest risk that we run in life is losing our health. There are many things in life that we can lose and recover from, but when you lose your health and it is gone, then it not only impacts you, but everyone around you. Becoming dependent on someone for health is a trap that many of us slowly fall into without realizing it. One goal of this chapter is to help you see that health independence not only can transform your own life and help you feel empowered to do more incredible things, but it also empowers everyone around you.

When you are mentally sharp, emotionally open, and your fitness is where it needs to be, you can perform the activities that you need to perform. This is when you really start to make the biggest impact. Health independence is a goal of mine because I have seen so many patients throughout the years who have been either dependent on a surgery, medication, or a doctor or health care provider to keep them healthy and mask their symptoms. Often, they have not taken their health into their own hands.

This book is a call to action to help you see that there is a clear path to find health independence. The first step begins with a commitment from you.

What parts of your health could use some fine-tuning?

Would you say that you are coachable?

Health independence is about learning, and we need coaches throughout this process. Health independence does not mean you are doing it on your own. Health independence means that you are finding mentors and people who will help give you guidance.

But, at the end of the day, are you willing to do the work of discovering your health again?

What are the three keys that you can focus on today that are going to be healthy habits that will lead to a bigger, better, healthier future?

1.

2.

3.

Medication and Surgery Trap

Medication is great when you have an infection or even possibly if there are no other solutions for your hypertension. It is better to take a drug than to have a stroke, right? However, the biggest thing we fall into is believing that medication is fixing a problem.

I have met with countless diabetics and the majority of them will say something like: *I'm not concerned about my diabetes because it is under control.*

I remind them that their diabetes is under control because they are on a diabetic medication. What would happen if they went off the medication is their blood sugars would not be balanced. Medication can suck us into believing we are healthy just because our doctor runs the numbers, and we do not have hypertension, high blood sugar, or our cholesterol looks normal. We think we are doing okay. Yet, this is how we become dependent on a medication. We do not dig in and find out why we developed the condition in the first place.

The other trap is we end up getting surgeries. There was a research done in the New Yorker magazine where they had surveyed three thousand individuals who had spinal surgeries, and they found that 72 percent of these individuals needed further surgery.[8] What happens with surgery is more than the scar tissue and damage; it is also the need for more surgery. With surgery comes rehab, physical therapy, more medication, and more down time. And, it masks our body's own ability to heal.

One of the biggest things that I have found in my patients who are in their nineties is that they avoid the trap of getting on medication. They are on zero or only a few medications, and they have had very few surgeries. Health dependence is hard because it is easy to start relying on a medication or a surgery for our health. Health independence is easy because that is when we start relying on natural methods and create an environment so that our bodies can heal themselves.

Doctors are Trained to Keep You Dependent

I often interview medical doctors, nurse practitioners, or physician assistants who come and work at our East West Health clinics, and one of the biggest breakthroughs for me was understanding the trap that the doctors are put in. I once interviewed a medical doctor, we will just call her Lisa. Lisa had worked in emergency medicine for over a decade. The pace was hurried, there was no down time, and what she

8   Groopman, Jerome. *A Knife in the Back.* Annals of Medicine, The New Yorker. April 8, 2002. newyorker.com/magazine/2002/04/08/a-knife-in-the-back.

found was that it was a conveyor belt bringing in the same people over and over again in the emergency room setting.

Now, this scenario is not anything new, but the problem was the only tools that Lisa was ever trained to use in medical school were pharmaceuticals. She could never sit down and talk to patients about lifestyle changes. She was never given tools in medical school to help dig in and motivate a person or to find the underlying causes that kept them coming back to the emergency room.

During our conversation, I was led to dive a little deeper into my own research, and Lisa started saying, "Yeah, actually all the medical schools are funded by the pharmaceutical companies."

If you look at any medical school throughout America, a pharmacy school is sitting right next to it. So, we have had doctors for almost eighty years now who are trained in pharmaceutical or chemical-driven medicine, and it is not a one-time medication. When you are prescribed a medication, how long will you be on the medication? Exactly, for life.

If you have hypertension, more than likely you are going to be taking hypertensive medication for as long as you live. This is exactly the way the doctors are trained. And, if your numbers look good, even though you are on the medication, then they feel like they have done their jobs.

One of the biggest obstacles to overcome in finding your health independence is moving beyond this model that there is a pill for every ill, or that you need medication. We have run thousands of labs in my East West Health clinics, and we have not found a single person to be *drug deficient*.

What medications are giving you side effects?

Breaking Free From Health Dependence

Imagine yourself off all your medications and feeling the best health of your life. I am forty years old at the time of this writing, and I feel ten times healthier than I did when I was twenty. Now imagine you are health independent, you have the right coaches and the right team around you, and you know exactly the steps you need to take to maintain incredible health.

Imagine your brain is working incredibly well, you can go on hikes, or do any physical activities that you like. You can pursue traveling dreams and working your dream job. Imagine how this feels and imagine what it could do for the quality of your life.

Now, the biggest step that you must take to break free from health dependence is to make it a daily habit to be as healthy as you can possibly be. It needs to be almost like your new religion where you focus every day on putting the right things in your mouth. Also focus on having the right thoughts and keeping your brain engaged in something novel that challenges you. Then, create and cultivate incredible relationships and amazing fitness.

One step I find useful in breaking free from health dependence is ordering the right labs. When I look at labs, I want to focus on five core pillars of health.

There are labs available that coincide with each one of these pillars:

1. The lab for the first pillar is a functional blood chemistry panel to show exactly what is going on internally.

2. The lab for the second pillar will look at genetics and can help find massive clues on where weak spots are. If we know where your weaknesses are, then we can make sure you are doing things to build them up and strengthen them.

3. The lab for the third pillar will look at gut health. We will want to do a stool test—whether that is with the company Viome, who we use, or Genova—and look at your gut and find out how healthy it is. This can show you if you have parasites or pathogenic fungus, or a bacteria overgrowth.

4. There are labs that show what foods are going to be good for you and what foods may not be so good for you. Every person needs their own nutritional roadmap.

5. The final pillar is brain health. For brain health, we can test neurotransmitters. There will also be factors of your brain health in your genetics.

6. Focusing on these key pillars of health will allow you to break free from any health dependence.

When was the last time you had your labs run?

PLANNING FOR THOSE OF US WHO LACK WILLPOWER

Progress begins by creating an environment that allows you to choose only once what your week will look like. Creating health then is planning and executing that plan. Your plan becomes stepping-stones that move you into a structured process that limits your choices so you can succeed.

Willpower does not work. Planning does not require any complicated tools. You can simply use a calendar or a journal.

Every week on Sunday, I like to sit down and plan. I calendar what days I will exercise hard with strength training or power Crossfit, go to yoga, mountain bike, or snowboard. I also have goals for my finances. I have goals for my amazing Go Wellness community and for my East West Health clinics. I plan for writing and recording projects, as well as time for research and seminars.

Then, I think about the friends I need to reach out to, and colleagues I want to contact. I plan for the upcoming events for my wife and my kids. And, I plan to do activities one on one with my kids and to have a weekly date night with my wife. These are all things that I set up every week with my assistant, and then I get daily reminders of what I need to do. I think you will find this to be one of the most meaningful practices for creating a great future for yourself.

Having a health coach can be one of the easiest ways to get the ball rolling. Feel free to email me at info@gowellness.com, and I will find the right coach for you.

What day each week will you plan your life?

Who will help you execute your plans?

Keeping Score and Measuring Outcomes in Fitness

There are many fitness apps available for our smart phones and devices we can wear from a Fitbit, to a Spire device, to a heart rate monitor. All these innovations are especially important because if you keep score and understand how well you are doing, then you will be able to measure your outcome. Our brains love a target.

Of these new breakthroughs, one of the fastest growing fitness franchises as of this writing is Orange Theory Fitness. They provide real time data as one of the key components of creating their fitness movement. I love looking up at the screen and seeing my heart rate and calories burned. It is also kind of fun to see how everyone else is doing. I like to see how much time I spend in the orange or in the red.

Using Orange Theory Fitness provides me clarity on how hard I'm working and allows me to set a new goal each time I use it. Some days I do not want to push as hard, but I always set a goal for seven hundred to one thousand calories burned per workout. I find this helps me achieve my desired fitness level.

For example, on yoga day I set my goals and then stay mindful so that I can do each pose without my balance being off. In my yoga practice, my goal is always to stay present in the room. The more present that I stay in the room, the more easily I can perform the various poses. For mountain biking day, I have goals for keeping score and measuring outcomes, and I like to see how fast I can complete certain trails.

If you have a smartphone, and I am assuming you do, one of the easiest places to start is setting a goal for daily steps.

How many steps are you going to take today?

How many times will you stop and take some nice deep breaths?

These practices will be some of the best things you can do to set an incredible future. I do not care if you are eighty years old, you can still create a bigger goal. With your scores and measurements, you can always create bigger goals for the future.

What activities are keeping you fit and how will you keep score?

How much improvement in your fitness level will you create?

Friends of All Ages

There are incredible people alive now who are in their nineties and hundreds. My wife's grandmother just turned 100 years old, and she is one of the most intelligent and witty human beings that I have ever met. She remembers using candles for light at night and having an outhouse for a bathroom.

It is phenomenal to think of all the wisdom you can learn from people who are a little older than you.

Whom in your life do you reach out to for advice and guidance?

Do you have friends or people who are older than you?

I find that the people who are older make the best mentors because they have already learned many of the hard lessons in life that I may not want to repeat. I also find that spending time with young people is incredibly interesting as well. I love having kids of my own because they bring their friends around, and I can ask their friends questions about what is happening on social media, or about the newest creative project they are working on.

My sons Jonah and Dominic have a friend named Zach. One evening, he and I were talking about our YouTube channels and were comparing notes. I found out he had nearly one hundred thousand followers—and he is a twelve-year-old kid!

I asked him, "How do you get so many followers? What are you doing that gets attention? What is your niche?"

Zach pieces different movies or different action themes together and has created a massive following. And, he did not even know it was a lot of people. I love working with people of all ages because they have different interests. I am interested in my twelve-year-old boys and my fourteen-year-old daughter. I am just as interested in their interests as I am in someone who is in their nineties.

I find that my patients who are in their nineties—or like my wife's grandmother, who is 100—have different ideas and different things they want to talk about. The more friends you can have of all age groups, the younger you are going to be. Having friends of varying ages will challenge your brain because your brain will develop a well-rounded view of the world. No matter what age you are, you can find friends who are a little older than you and a little younger. Simply having some conversations with them is a great way to set yourself up for a great future with friends.

Economic Independence for Health Independence

Leaving the comforts of home and finding ways to produce income is a rite of passage into adulthood. It is an empowering time in life. At the age of seventeen, I started a concrete business. By the age of eighteen I had enough money to pay for college with money I had saved up from that job combined with the income I was able to save from working on our family farm.

While in college, I was able to continue operating a small construction business. It was a lot of hard work going to school full-time and working full-time. But, the feeling of economic independence made me feel healthier and happier. I felt proud and knew that I could tackle any problem that came to me in life.

Living and not being economically independent can be particularly challenging. One of my mentors for my financial life is Garrett Gunderson from Wealth Factory. They train their clients on how to create economic independence. I highly recommend finding a coach who can help you no matter where you are financially. It's time to start thinking about a long future where you enjoy your work so much that you don't see retirement as an option.

Retirement is a thing of the past. I think the world is becoming so much more interesting, and we have so much more to do. You will want to keep creating value, no matter what age you are. When you create value, you create economic independence. The more economic independence you have, the easier it is for you to have your health independence because finances do not stress you out.

What are you doing now to create economic independence?

Imagine yourself in a position where you are 100 years old, but you are still able to generate revenue by adding value and serving a community. Whether that is by presently working within your enterprise, or other people are doing it for you—you are setting the vision. Economic independence starts with changing the mindset that we only add value until we are sixty-five and then we check out. Economic independence is a new mindset where you know you always have value to add, and you can always generate and bring in revenue.

How many careers will you have?

Who knows, maybe some of you will live to live to be 200 or 180. It is hard to say, but I know that we are going to be living a long time now that we have the tools for continued health.

YOUR VISION FOR YOUR BIGGER, BETTER, HEALTHIER FUTURE

Any large, meaningful task in life requires a clear vision. If you do not have clarity, you are going to have confusion. Any time that you are confused about what you want your future to look like, then other people pull you into their agenda—that will become your future.

If you can create a vision for what you want your life to look like and how you want your health to be, you can make the choice right now that will enhance your health daily. Or, maybe you are at the place where that is not really your thing. But, no matter what you choose, create a vision for a bigger, better, healthier future.

I think about how much better life is. We have over 7 billion people on the planet, and still the most valuable resource on the planet is humans—you and me. It is *you;* we need you around to lend your talents and creativity. We need you healthy and alert.

The more that we grow as individuals, the more we grow together. We still have a lot of work to do, but if you can create a vision for your own personal life—one that you can direct—then, your vision can expand and connect with many other people throughout the world. In the next five years, we are going to have nearly 7 billion people online. That means the entire world will be connected. Right now, we are not anywhere near that, but in a very short time we will all be connected.

What does your future look like?

If you have a bigger, better, and healthier future planned, then you will help other people create their bigger, better, and healthier future as well.

Making Health A Daily Process

Each day, you have a choice. That choice is: *Will I do things to create and cultivate better health in my body?* Now, I spent a lot of time earlier in this book talking about stem cell proliferation. Stem cells are a new form of life and energy in your body. Each day, if you can stimulate and bring some new health and light to your cells as they turn over—as you have 300 million cells dying every minute—the stem cells that come in to replenish the cells that have died will create much better health.

This means that every minute of every day we need to be looking at what we can do to enhance our health. This may mean doing something as simple as pausing and taking a few deep breaths throughout your work day. It can be something as simple as taking the stairs instead of the elevator. You can park your car further away or ride your bike to work. Or, you can walk to work.

Creating an environment that leads to healthier choices makes everything easier.

There are so many things that we can do to improve our lives. But, when you look at creating a daily process for your health, you need someone there to hold you accountable. As mentioned before, health coaches are phenomenal, and you also have technology that you can use. You can easily use your smartphone to remind you of when you need to do the things that you committed to do daily.

The first step in making health a daily process is to carve out time every morning. For your morning mindset, spend five minutes visualizing how your day is going to go.

Visualize:

- What you will put into your mouth in the day
- What your exercise routine is going to look like
- Yourself connecting with people
- Bringing your best foot forward in your daily interactions

This is the starting place. Step two is making the commitment that you are going to do these things and remind yourself of them throughout the day. This is how you will make health a daily process, and if you make it daily process, then it will become a lifetime process.

Small Steps Lead to Massive Outcomes

One of my favorite patients, we will call him Donald, had a desire to lose 120 pounds. Now, the problem with Donald is that he had osteoarthritis in his knees and was facing a total knee replacement, but he could not get the surgery until he lost weight. Also, he did not want to do the surgery.

Donald first took small steps. The first thing we did for Donald was inject umbilical cord stem cells into his knees, and it gave him some pain relief. Then, we put him on an exercise program, changed his nutrition, and changed the way he was thinking about his life.

I remember at month three of working with Donald, he had already lost thirty pounds. That was phenomenal. He was elated, but then he decided to take a few days off from his new habits.

Donald said, "I am going on vacation."

He went on vacation, and he gained almost every single pound he had lost in just one two-week vacation.

We saw him after his vacation and we said, "Okay, let's sit down and figure out what needs to happen so we can get you back on track. Let's just take small steps. These are going to lead you to your biggest outcomes."

So, Donald started keeping a food journal. He started exercising every day and did not take a day off. He did not cheat one day on this food, and he followed the time restrictive eating schedule. And within a year, Donald had lost 120 pounds. What I found is that we had to simplify, not complicate things.

So, whenever you are looking to make a massive change in your life, remember that the simplest thing we did for

Donald is we said, "Let's get you out of pain so you can move your body."

The second simplification we did is we said to Donald, "Let's try time-restrictive eating."

We put him on an eight-hour window and that was the only time he could eat, and we gave him the right foods to eat but we said, "As long as you are eating on an eight-hour window you are going to have a little more leeway."

The third thing we did is we made sure he was exercising every day, and that he was meeting his benchmarks. We gave him simple goals to reach every day so that he felt that he was always accomplishing something.

When you feel on a day-to-day basis: *Yes, I have accomplished something today,* then you start having breakthroughs and massive outcomes in your health.

What Does Health Independence Look Like to You?

Health independence is a journey that we are all on. It must be a daily process because we never know if we are going to get in an accident or have something severe happen to us at any given time. Life is fragile. While we are empowered to look for our health independence, think about what it means to you.

What do you want your life to look like, and how do you want it to feel?

Do you have pain right now?

Let's look at that. Pain that goes unresolved usually grows worse. A baseline for health independence is being free from pain.

The next necessary step is to look at labs. We must really dig in and focus on the core of health.

We will focus on the health of your:

- Brain
- Gut
- Hormones
- Nutrition
- Genetics

And then, you can really dig in and say: *Okay, am I healthy in all the compartments of my life?*

Look at your relationships. Are your relationships where they need to be, where you would like them to be?

How is your relationship with your spirituality?

How is your relationship with your family—with your loved ones?

Are there any unresolved issues?

Are there relationships you need to end?

All these things need to be looked at when it comes to health independence. Because health independence, to me, is feeling empowered to take action and do the things that I want to do at an optimal level with the people I love being with. Yet, health independence is going to look differently for every single one of us.

Think about these ideas:

- Maybe you could live a lot longer than you originally planned.

- There are a multitude of relationships that you can have.

- There are opportunities for economic independence.

When you start cultivating these ideas, then we can sit back and simply write out what your health independence looks like to you.

Action: Set a timer on your phone to take five minutes and write out what health independence looks like.

How does that feel, what does it look like?

What are the criteria that need to be met for you to have your health independence?

Starting here is where you can experience the breakthroughs of your life. You will achieve and maintain because you will learn more about your own health than anyone else could ever teach you by observing. I hope this has given you an insight and a perspective like no other. One that shines a light on a beautiful path that can lead to tremendous health for the future.

Conclusion

I am honored that you have come this far in the book. I congratulate you and appreciate the journey that you have taken with me to create bigger and better health and to also create a better future for us all. The next steps are important because this is the implementation time; this is when you can start to think about the ways you would like to transform your own life.

The first thing that you can do right out of the gate is start creating the relationships that can really serve you and bring you to a much bigger and better place. The second thing is to find a health care practitioner who can take the time to understand what your individual needs are. One of the best resources that you have available are the stem cells health centers or call one of our East West Health clinics. We will dive in and explore any areas of vulnerability because my goal is to help you to live to be 120 and beyond.

I want you to be the ones breaking the world record when it comes to longevity. We cannot do that if we have any type of malfunctions or imbalances in our body. The purpose of this book is to give you clarity—to give you a map—but most importantly, to help you create a bigger vision for your own health and your own future. The best way to do this is by charting out the course you want.

I recommend starting with six deep breaths. This has been found in Japanese research to change your state of being. Take six nice, deep breaths, nice and easy, then start writing down your vision for the future. Then, write down all the names of the people you already know who could help you create a team that will help you accomplish your biggest goals for your future health.

There will be many nuances to navigate, and biology is not ever as simplified as we sometimes make it out to be. As you have read through this book, I have given you some simple solutions that you can start implementing into your life right away. If you need help on your journey, we are always here.

Illness is something that goes unrecognized in today's busy chaotic world. One of the most gratifying things is when you can just be still for a moment and feel your body—feel the energy that is in it, the light that you have been blessed with, and take some time to really appreciate it. Health is about embracing and appreciating all the opportunities that come in life.

Sometimes, opportunities look like pitfalls. I have had some of my deepest learning experiences come out of some of the hardest circumstances of my life. I believe that you can relate. No one is getting out of this life without some type of struggle or learning opportunity.

Take a minute to find your inner stillness. Appreciate everything around you day to day, moment by moment.

Cultivating internal depth and wisdom can be one of the greatest sources of healing for you. It will also help transform the neurotransmitters in your brain. You will begin to experience a nervous system that is non-agitated.

With stillness, you will not feel like you are missing out on every little opportunity. Without stillness, we can end up in the scarcity mentality where we feel like we must do everything at once and for everybody else. If we are in the scarcity mentality, then we are going to miss out on some great opportunities.

Realize that your health is right inside. If you take one minute every day, even right now, and appreciate the health that you have been blessed with, this forms the foundation for you to build a much bigger, deeper, and healthier future. I want to express my deep gratitude and appreciation for you taking the opportunity to read this book. I believe that the more people embrace their healing journey, the healthier our planet, communities, families, friendships, and relationships will be. This will help us propel into a much more exciting, bigger future where we can all collaborate and work together.

We can all find meaningful ways to connect. I want to thank and congratulate you for going through this journey. I am here for you, even if it is in spirit.

Finally, I want to share my love and deep respect for this thing we call life.

Next Steps

People often ask me: *Regan, how can we work together?*

Working together can be as simple as sending an email to me at info@gowellness.com or visiting Yourhealthyself.com and leaving your information. I would be honored to hear from you.

I would also love to hear your success stories and to be a part of your health care team. I feel that we are looking for like-minded people, and the fact that you are reading this book means that we would most likely have a great relationship together. The best way to find me is through email. You can also find my clinics on the web at acueastwest.com. Give us a call to set up a consultation.

For those of you who are looking to have regenerative therapy such as stem cell therapy—don't wait any longer. We can help. My goal is to help you end your pain and chronic disease. Please find me on YouTube: Regan Archibald.

If you would like to become more engaged, find us on our East West Health YouTube channel where you will find many videos on a variety of different health topics. They will help you stay motivated or they might just not help at all— who knows?

You can also listen to my podcasts, Go Wellness Radio and *Your Healthy Self* on iTunes. One of the best avenues you can use to stay connected with this vision, this purpose that I have of transforming your health and your life, is to listen to the podcasts as you're commuting to work or as you are working out. I think it will lend a little more insight to the topics in this book.

Lastly, I welcome you to join us for our 5-Day and 100-Day challenges. You can access the challenges for this book on the website: Yourhealthyself.com.

About the Author

Regan Archibald, Lac, CSSAc, Functional Medicine Provider, is the Founder of the award-winning clinic, East West Health, which has four clinics in the state of Utah that employ the best of both eastern and western trained doctors. He is also the Founder of Go Wellness, which is the industry leader in creating a new genre in healthcare with research-based programs in acupuncture, functional medicine, and stem cell therapy.

Regan is a prolific writer, podcast host, energized speaker, and instructor for The Lotus Institute and Go Wellness. He has created over fifteen training courses to educate and inspire people to find their health independence. He has advanced post-graduate training in stem cell therapy, functional medicine, corporate wellness, and personalized nutrition. Regan is a sought-after speaker and has shared the stage with some of the world's top leaders in healthcare. He has addressed Fortune 500 companies like American Express and Parker Hannifin.

The East West Health clinics have helped over 60,000 patients since opening in 2004, and his Go Wellness training programs have inspired well over one thousand healthcare practitioners. Regan believes that the future of medicine arrives when doctors and healers become teachers and mentors. He sees a future where advanced testing and treatments help a talented team of healthcare providers uncover and treat disease patterns before they ever present themselves. He helps people love the way they feel about their health and their life, and believes that the deepest form of service that he can provide is one where he shows others their own path to freedom in their health.

Regan's free time is spent enjoying the mountains in Park City, Utah, where he lives with his amazing wife and kids, Zoe, Dominic, and Jonah. He enjoys traveling, mountain biking, snowboarding, yoga, and doing extreme experiments with his own mind and body. He has read two books every week for the last ten years.

Regan deeply appreciates and credits his success to his amazing patients who have helped him uncover the truth faster than any book, and to his incredible mentors who have been coaching him from the beginning.